I Remembered Job

Demetrio Maestas

I Remembered Job

This book is written to provide information and motivation to readers. Its purpose is not to render any type of psychological, legal, or professional advice of any kind. The content is the sole opinion and expression of the author, and not necessarily that of the publisher.

Copyright © 2020 by Demetrio Maestas

All rights reserved. No part of this book may be reproduced, transmitted, or distributed in any form by any means, including, but not limited to, recording, photocopying, or taking screenshots of parts of the book, without prior written permission from the author or the publisher. Brief quotations for noncommercial purposes, such as book reviews, permitted by Fair Use of the U.S. Copyright Law, are allowed without written permissions, as long as such quotations do not cause damage to the book's commercial value. For permissions, write to the publisher, whose address is stated below.

Printed in the United States of America.

ISBN 978-1-953150-01-1 (Paperback)
ISBN 978-1-953150-02-8 (Digital)

Lettra Press books may be ordered through booksellers or by contacting:

Lettra Press LLC
30 N Gould St. Suite 4753
Sheridan, WY 82801, USA
1 307-200-3414 | info@lettrapress.com
www.lettrapress.com

Contents

Acknowledgments 7
Introduction 9
Prologue 11

Chapter One	"The Birth Of Richard And Move To New Mexico" 13	
Chapter Two	"Richard And Sarah's Terrible Tragedy" 17	
Chapter Three	"John Begins To Oppose Bob" 19	
Chapter Four	"Bob's Family Starts Working Full Time" 21	
Chapter Five	"The Beginning Of Bob's Family Trails" 23	
Chapter Six	"John's Lack Of Understanding Faith" 25	
Chapter Seven	"The Results Of God's People Working" 27	
Chapter Eight	"Beginning Of David's Trails" 29	
Chapter Nine	"God Of Mercy And Comfort" 31	

Chapter Ten	"John's Concern For Bob Neglecting His Business"	33
Chapter Eleven	"More Trails For Bob's Family"	35
Chapter Twelve	"More Trails For David"	37
Chapter Thirteen	"John's Concern For Bob's Business"	41
Chapter Fourteen	"John Takes Control Of Bobs Business"	43
Chapter Fifteen	"Work For The Lord Doing Great"	45
Chapter Sixteen	"The Beginning Of Bob's Family Turning On Him"	49
Chapter Seventeen	"The Testing Of Bob's Faith"	51
Chapter Eighteen	"Bob Defends God's Mercies"	53
Chapter Nineteen	"The Turnaround"	55
Chapter Twenty	"Bob's Victory Lap"	59

Disclaimer

This story is based on fiction. Any similarities between the characters and business's and actual people is a mere coincidence.

Acknowledgments

MY THANKS TO my grandson, Benjamin, for helping me in my writing. Even though I learned how to type in high school, it had been years that I have done any typing. I also thank my parents, for leading in the narrow path. They taught me to always rely on the Lord. My English teacher always told me I have the talent to be a writer. Thanks to her encouragement, this came into fruition over fifty years later. May this story encourage Christian people to help the less fortunate. There are so many things that can be accomplished if Christian people work together.

Introduction

IT WAS IN the mid nineteen eighties' when I came to realize that just being a church member was not enough.

I was born in Holman New Mexico, a small northern New Mexico community. I grew up in a big family. I was the youngest of twelve. but my parents taught us to always remember that we are to live a Christian life. After graduating from High School, I began to realize that I had to start thinking about my future. It was very hard to think that soon I was going to be on my own and. Being that I was the youngest, it was hard for my Patents to let me go. I knew that if I wanted to get ahead with my life I had to relocate. I decided to move in with my older brother and sister in law. So, I made my move to Barstow California. Since I was the youngest my Parents considered me as their Baby, but they gave me their blessing, and with a lot of sadness I made my move to Barstow Califormia. I remember how sad I felt the day I left my parents.

At the age of twenty-three I got married. My wife Mary and I were the proud parents of two Children Rosalynn and Timothy. Even though we were believers it was hard for us to find a Church because Mary was Catholic, and I was Presbyterian it was hard for us to find a Church where we both felt comfortable, so we wondered aimlessly. One day a neighbor of ours invited us to her Church. Mary accepted and attended First Baptist Church of Barstow. I couldn't go because I had to work that Sunday, so Mary went by herself. When I came home that evening she was excited that it was such a friendly Church. We started attending and finally became members.

After being members of first Baptist, we had to relocate, so we found a Church that we both liked. We got very involved with First Southern Baptist Church of Apple Valley, where I eventually became a Deacon our new Church. The Deacon body decided to become more involved with helping the less fortunate in the Community. Along with other area Churches we started an organization which we called Hope Line. We found out that we must do what Christ commended us to do. Math 25:35 says I was hungry, and you gave me something to eat Math 35:45 as much as you have done to one of the least of these you have done it unto Me. While living in Albuquerque I found and joined Sage Brush Community Church Sage Brush is a Christ loving Bible teaching Church. So, I realized that being a Church member is not enough

Prologue

THE BOOK OF Job is the story of a man that loved God and denied evil. He went through hard times, but never denied God. God allowed Satan to test Job by removing His family and wealth, but he could not touch Job.

Chapter One

"The Birth Of Richard And Move To New Mexico"

RICHARD ANDREW WAS born to John and Rose Andrew in small farming community in central Wisconsin. It was the year 1927 doing the Recession, but John and Rose came from wealthy parents. So even though there was a lot of poverty around them, they lived a good life. When Richard was six his brother Tom was born two years later his sister Angie was born. John and Rose raised their Children to love the Lord. The whole family were always involved in their Church and Community. The children were involved in Children Church activities and helping the community cope with the poor people suffering from the recession. John and Rose always taught their Children to live by Grace and love in the Lord Jesus Christ. The Andrew family were always involved in doing volunteer work in their community.

John and Rose had two other siblings, Tom and Angie. As the children were growing up the family were involved in their Church and Community. The children were also involved with boys and girls clubs and other children activities in their School. John and Rose were always teaching their children to live by the Grace and love of the Lord Jesus Christ. They showed their love by volunteering in doing charity work in their community. They

Demetrio Maestas

were very wealthy. They owned a very large Dairy Farm and, they owned a lot of property.

They always wanted to expand and increase their wealth. One day when their children grew up, they found out that there was a dairy farm for sale in New Mexico. They knew very little about New Mexico. They learned that New Mexico is in the Southwestern part of the Country. New Mexico is called the land of enchantment because of its topography. A person can be in the desert and within thirty minutes he can be in the wilderness. After inquiring more about the State of New Mexico they decided to learn more about the property. After six months of learning about the property they decided to inquire about the purchase price. After they found how much the price of the farm they started negotiating the purchase price after they agreed on the price with a lot of Prayer they decided to buy it. To Bob and Rose was a new adventure to own a business in another State. Bob decided to go see what their new business looked like, so he decided to go see what they had purchased. So, he took a long trip to New Mexico. As he arrived in Albuquerque, the first thing he noticed was the different culture. He noticed that a lot of people spoke Spanish, but they were very friendly. He also noticed that there was a lot of Native American and Spanish architecture. When he. visited the dairy farm he was glad to see what they invested on. There was a lot of property around it. The barns needed some work and the whole farm had to be modernized. Over all he was glad for what they purchased. When he returned to Wisconsin, he decided that a family member would have to move to New Mexico to oversee the daily operations of the dairy. Since Richard at twenty-five years old, and had finished school majoring in Business administration, they decided that he move to New Mexico to oversee the operation of the farm.

At first Richard objected but his parents convinced him to take that challenge. As the plane was arriving in Albuquerque he noticed the Sandia Mountains He right away knew that New Mexico is a lot different than Wisconsin. When Richard arrived in Albuquerque he also found out how different the culture was in New Mexico. He noticed how laid back the people were as he drove around the area he found out how friendly the people were. He also noticed the different foods and accent they had. There were a lot of Spanish speaking people. As he drove around Albuquerque he began to like the place. He soon found out that he will like living here Two weeks after he found living quarters, he started looking for a Church. He was raised in Church. He found it very important to find a Church that he could be involved in. The Church had to have a good Mission program. After visiting several Churches, he settled on one located in down town Albuquerque. After several weeks of attending the Church he started making friends. He met a young Lady. To him it was love at first sight. The young Ladies Name was Sarah. Sarah was bilingual, the Daughter of Juan and Dolores Baca. Several weeks after he Joined the Church he started dating Sarah. He called his parents to let them know that he found the Mate he will spend the rest of his life with. As he asked Juan and Dolores for their Daughters hand in marriage. The date was set for the wedding. He to get used to the different culture the Baca family had He also had to get used to the spicy food they ate. After six months of dating they decided to get married. The whole Andrew family plus a bunch of friends came to the wedding. They liked the different ceremony and wedding dance. They danced a special dance called la Marsha. A year after their marriage they had their first Child. They were so happy that it was the first of their family they decided to name their first Child Robert. They started calling him Bob. Two years later they were blessed with a second Child they named him John. Richard and Sarah raised their children with a lot of love. As the boys were growing up the whole family were involved with their Church and community. In seven years, they decided to name the businesss after their sons. They named the dairy farm B&J dairies. They became very prosperous. Beside the dairy the named the trucking company J&B trucking. They also invested in stocks and bonds, plus a property in south eastern New Mexico. As Bob and John grew up, they had different ideas about their view on life. Bob was sixteen years old he was always involved with the Church. He was always helping poor people in the community. John on the other hand at fourteen was always with His Dad tending to the family business. When Bob was twenty and John was eighteen they started dating young ladies from their Church. Bobs girl was named Rebecca. Johns girl was Judy. Both Rebecca and Judy loved the Lord and their Church. They were always involved with Church activities since they were growing up.

    Bob and Rebecca were the first to marry. John and Judy married three months later. At the age of twenty-seven Bob and Rebecca were parents of five siblings, three Boys and two Girls. The three Boys were named Brian, Robert and David. The Girls were named Mary and Rose. John and Judy had three boys Kenneth, Troy and Ray. Both the families had their children grow up with Christ being the center of their lives.

Chapter Two

"Richard And Sarah's Terrible Tragedy"

BOB AND REBECA'S family were always involved in many community and Church affairs such as Catholic charities and Salvation Army. John and His family had different ideas on how things God wanted them to do, they were always working to expand their business. Other than their business John and his family thought very little about what is going on in their community. Richard and Sarah were so glad to see their boys grow up and have families of their own. They were sad when they lost Richards parents about nine months apart. As Richard and Sarah saw their children grow up and have children of their own, they were content that the Lord has been good to them. One day other than going to their parent's funeral in Wisconsin after several years without a vacation, they had been living in Albuquerque for about twenty-five years. Richard and Sarah decided to take three weeks off to go see their friends in southern New Mexico. Their friends were originally from Wisconsin. Since they were living in New Mexico, other than the Albuquerque area they have never been to any other parts of New Mexico. They had never seen the property they owned. They also wanted to go visit the missions they were supporting. They decided to leave Bob in charge of the Ministry and John in charge of the business. They trusted their sons to see that everything went well. After saying their good buys, they started their trip. Other than the Albuquerque area, they knew very little about New Mexico. They didn't realize how big New Mexico is. After getting on the interstate they were content that they had such a wonderful family. Both their sons were married to God loving Ladies. And they were raising their grand Children to be good responsible Christian citizens. About fifty miles east of Albuquerque, Richard got distracted and lost control of the car. They went on to the west bound lanes of the freeway and met head on with a big rig truck. They both claimed their victory and went to be with the Lord. People don't realize how quick death comes and they have stand before Christ. When they left they were so happy? They never got to see their friends, but the Lord had other plans for them. When the family got the news, they were devastated. The entire community was in shock for what had happened to the Andrew family. They left behind their two son and their wife's plus eight Grand Children. They left many memories. They were always involved with the Church and community charitable organizations. People from Wisconsin and all around the Albuquerque area attended the funeral. After the funeral the family had to adjust their lives without their parents. Richard and Sarah left so many memories, but after many days of sadness they were content that one day they will become one big happy family in Heaven. They left their marks in many Church and Community charitable organizations. It was a sad moment to see them go, but God needed them more.

Ephesians 6:10 states that we are to be strong in the Lord.

Chapter Three

"John Begins To Oppose Bob"

IT TOOK OVER three years for the Andrew family to function without their parents. Bob and his family continued with the Ministry, while John and his family concentrated more on the family business. It was a cool spring morning; Bobs family had just finished breakfast and were getting ready for a busy day. Bob went to his office to figure the schedule for the day. they had so many things on their schedule. Bob was waiting to hear from a new Church that wanted to join their effort. The rest of the family started getting ready. Besides the Ministry they had to see what to do about B&J Dairy. The doorbell rang David opened the door and saw his uncle John waiting outside. David was startled to see his uncle John with a mean look on his face. John looked very frustrated and had a stern look on his face. with a mean voice he asked for his brother. when Bob came out John confronted him. Bob, we have a problem I got a call from the dairy farm Forman. He told me that there were a lot of problems with the farm. Bob, we must concentrate more on our business. Some of the barns are in bad shape. and they need to be repaired. Bob, we need new and more modern milking machines. If we don't modernize the dairy farm will fall behind. We have a lot of competition that will take over if we can't deliver our product. We need to rebuild our barns and buy more nutritious food for our cows. We also need to buy more milking cows. My brother you need to start paying more attention to your business, instead of spending your time with the Church and Charitable organizations. Bob, I know how our parents felt about helping the needy. and I understand how you feel about the less fortunate, but you also have to understand that family comes first. John, I understand your concern, and I know you care about the less fortunate. but you must understand that we must take a stand and do the work that God wants from us. My family and I think it's very important to serve God.1st Cor 3:9:" for we are God's fellow workers; you are God's field God's building" So since We are Gods fellow workers, We have to take the challenge and be the salt of the Earth, and we are committed to do the Lords work. My brother we can do many things through God who strengthens us. As we look around our community, there are so many things that can be done to help our Brothers and Sisters. John, we must listen to Christ who gave us the commandment to love one another.

John, I know you are a believer, but you are more interested On you and your earthly riches then helping the needy. Bob it's a nice thing you're doing by helping people in need. I know you are a compassionate person, but you also have to understand that your business takes precedence over your Charity work. If you keep up with your ridiculous endeavor. I have no alternative but to go on my own. Brother, I have to protect my own interests. John remember John 3;16" for God so loved the world, that He sent his only Son that who so ever believeth in Him shall not perish but have ever lasting life" When we see what He did for us we have to do His work. We know that He will provide for us and He will provide all our needs.

Chapter Four

"Bob's Family Starts Working Full Time"

IT WAS EARLY summer; Bob and his family have been busy looking for things to help less fortunate people all around the community. John and his family on the other hand were content just going to Church on Sundays. John thought that all God wanted was to be Worshiped on Sunday. Gal.5:13" You my Brothers and Sisters were called to be free. But do not use your freedom to indulge the flesh; Rather serve one another humbly in love" John and his family knew very little about serving God. Bob and his family decided to commit themselves to devote more of their time to doing the Lords work, so they decided to start working full time. David and Andrew were put in charge of overseeing the building of a new warehouse. The warehouse must be big enough to accommodate furniture clothing and have room for a big walk in refrigerator. The warehouse will be built on one hundred and fifty acres donated by Bob and his family. Rebecca was put in charge of training people from the area Church's on how to bring Gods love to the less fortunate people, by teaching them that God is love and is ready to come into their lives. Rose job was to train volunteers to work in homeless shelters. Robert and Mary's job were to encourage young homeless people to get educated so they can become responsible members of their community. The whole family were united in helping the less fortunate share in the blessings that God gives. Everybody deserves to Share in Gods blessings.

Math. 9:38" There for pray earnestly to the Lord of the Harvest to send out laborers into His Harvest" This means that God has to have servants to accomplish His work. One day John started getting concerned that Bob and his family were busy working for the Lord the Lord and ignoring their business, so he decided to confront Bob. He wanted to know what is going to happen to their business if they keep on working for the less fortunate. Bob you and your family are letting your business go into ruin to help people you don't even know. Bob looked at John and with a smile, knowing that John only thought about enriching himself and ignoring the fact that God needs His people to work for the less fortunate. John didn't realize that with God in control nothing is going to go wrong. John no matter what obstacles we go through we can overcome them with God being the center of our lives.

When God is in control everything works together for Good.

Chapter Five

"The Beginning Of Bob's Family Trails"

BOB AND HIS family were having a lot of success with their endeavors. They knew that God was on their side. Everything they did was done by the faith in the Lord Jesus Christ. With a lot of prayer, they had a lot of volunteers that were joining the effort and bring good results. They were always looking for more ways to increase their mission. As Bob was looking around he found out that there was a small motel for sell close to down town. The first thing that went through his mind was how many people would be able to have homes if the motel could be turned into small apartments. It would be a big boost in increasing their mission. After inspecting the motel, he found out that with some work they could turn it into about thirty small apartments. It would be ideal for small families to get back on their feet. Bob decided to buy the motel and the property around it. He found a lot of volunteers with carpenter experience, so they started remodeling to turn them into apartments. The Lord was blessing Bob and His family with a lot of volunteers. They had volunteers to work in homeless shelters and soup kitchens.

It has been twenty-six years since Richard and Sarah went to be with the Lord. Bob and his family continued what their parents had started. John and his family were also working, but they were working on enriching themselves. Late summer was the beginning of our troubles. The Beatitudes in Mathew chapter five states "blessed are the merciful: for they shall be shown mercy" it was late august when the family began to have problems. Rebecca woke up at five am and was not feeling good. For about three months She noticed waking up feeling dizzy. She had numbness on her hands and feet. It had been several days that she was getting worse. It looked like she was losing her strength, but she saw how good things were going that she didn't want to let Bob know about her problems. When Bob found out he stared at the wall and was very disappointed that his wife did not trust him. He loves his wife and will do whatever it takes to see that his wife is in the best of health. He was not happy that she kept her problem from him. Her Doctor diagnosed her with type two diabetes. He did was put her on insulin and also put her on a strict diet. She also needed a lot of rest. That meant that she had to curtail a lot of her activities. Bob had Mary take over most of his wife's duties, also some of the people from their Church volunteered to help so that work will go on. The Apostle Paul did not give up His Ministry when he had setbacks. Satan is always putting obstacles on Gods workers, but the Lord always provides ways to work around them. When Christ instructed the Apostles to spread the Gospel they didn't stop when they were suffering persecution. So, no matter what Satan tries to do to Bob and his family they are going to keep on doing God's work.

Chapter Six

"John's Lack Of Understanding Faith"

WHILE BOB AND his family were busy working with the Church and other charitable organizations, and volunteers from all around the community were busy spreading Gods Love. John and his family were ignoring the progress being done and were always finding way to enrich them self's. He had no desire to help his brother, nephews, and Churches working for the Lord. Instead of helping his brother he was concerned that Bob and his family were busy with the ministry and ignoring his business. John did not understand anything about the Lord. To him his duty was to go to Church on Sundays and the Lord will take care of everything. When a rich young ruler asked Christ what he had to do to achieve eternal life. Jesus told him to sell all he had and give to the poor and he would receive rich's in Heaven.

John was confused and did not understand how God works. Bob explained to John that we must walk by faith. Faith is believing in something you don't see, but you know it's going to bring results. John faith is having confidence in God even when you don't see Him, but knowing he is always with you. You can find out what faith is when you start reading scripture. Rom.5:2-3" 2" Through whom also we have obtained our introduction by Faith into which stand and exult in hope of the Glory of God 3" and not only this, but we also exult in our tribulation, know that tribulation brings about perseverance" You will find that God provides all our needs. John just pray that the Holy Spirit will guide you, and God will be with you and never leave you no matter what happens here on earth. You can find out what faith is when you start reading Scripture. You will find that God provides all our needs. John just pray that the Holy Spirit will guide you and God will never live you or forsake you.

Chapter Seven

"The Results Of God's People Working"

PROVERBS 3:5" TRUST in the all your heart and lean not onto your own understanding" In the meantime, after much prayer and hard work, our endeavor was bringing fast results. We could see the Glory of God coming to the needy and less fortunate. After nine months of hard work Bob was proud of the accomplishment that was done in just a few months. The neighborhood Churches started collecting food furniture, clothing. It was amazing to see God loving people united in the purpose of making the community a better place to live. Catholic Charities and their volunteers were helping people find jobs in poverty-stricken neighborhoods and helping the Elderly who had no form of transportation meet their medical appointments. The Albuquerque Ministerial association were helping low income people find housing and serving meals in homeless shelters. Bob was asking God to make John understand that we must do what He commended us to do, that is to love one another. We demonstrate love by being His servants.

Chapter Eight

"Beginning Of David's Trails"

IT WAS SIX am Monday morning, after a good night's sleep, David woke up and thanked the Lord for another day. Bob and his family have been in the Ministry for several years. David was proud of what has been accomplished. He started thinking about how to make the warehouse more useful for the Ministry. As he was getting up he started making plans for the day. After breakfast he decide to call his brother so that he could meet him, so they can make plans on how to make room for more all the donations that were coming in. When he got ready to go to the warehouse he decided to call some volunteers to help rearrange furniture to make more room for what was coming in that day. He was proud that Brian and he were given the responsibility to oversee that the warehouse was always full of furniture, clothing and the food in the refrigerator was always rotated. David always had to make sure that there was enough room for everything that was being donated. When he got ready to go to the warehouse. He decided to call some volunteers to help in making more room for the donated items that were going to be delivered that day.

Psalm 25:4" Show me the right path, oh Lord; point out the road for me to follow" As he was driving to the warehouse a lot of things were going through his mind. He was so thankful that God was letting him be part of all the wonderful things that were being accomplished. There were so many people that were being helped. As he approached the inter section of tenth and central, he didn't realize that he wasn't going to able to stop when the signal light turned red. As he went into the middle of the intersection he saw a blue pickup truck coming right at him He was tee boned on the passenger side.

Even though couple in the pickup were wearing their seat belts and there was air bag deployment, they were still seriously hurt. With the shock of the collision David realized that he was hurt. The first thing David did was call for God to help him. Psalm16:1-2" Protect me God because I take refuge in You.2. I say to the Lord, you are my Lord, apart from You I have nothing good" His right leg was hurting bad and he was having trouble breathing. When the Paramedics came the first thing they did was put David on oxygen. When they got to the Hospital Bob and Rebecca were notified about the accident by Emergency room personal. Psalms 121:1-2" lift up my eyes to the mountains, from where does my help come from? My help comes from the Lord. 2. My help comes from the Lord which made Heaven and Earth" Bob and Rebecca started praying for the victims of the accident. Bob notified Pastor Gerald from their Church. On their way to the Hospital Bob asked God to be with them in their hour of need. The whole family met at the Hospital and were devastated. Bob remembered how he lost his parents. It would be devasting if he lost his son. The first thing that came to his mind was that God is in control. 2nd Cor. 1:3-4 says" blessed be God even the Father of our Lord Jesus Christ, the Father of Mercies, the God of comfort; who comforts us in all tribulations, that we may be able to comfort them which are in trouble, by the comfort that we ourselves are comforted by God"

The emergency room Doctors informed the family that the prognoses for David was not good. He had a punctured lung; his leg was fractured several places. He also had three cracked ribs. The Doctors also informed them that David is going to be laid up for a year and maybe more.

"Why does God allow us to go through trials and tribulations"

Chapter Nine

"God Of Mercy And Comfort"

AFTER BEING ASSURED that David will eventually regain his health and will again be a Soldier for the Lord, we must figure out how to help David deal with his afflictions. Romans 8:28" says that God loves His workers and works all things together for good to those who love God, to those who are called according to His purpose" So, God allowed this to happen to David for a Divine purpose. We know that with God on our side will have many blessings coming to us So, to emphasize, 2nd Cor.1:3-4 "All praise goes to God the father of our Lord Jesus Christ. God is a merciful Father the source of all comfort, for He comforts us, so we can comfort others"

After pastor Gerald got the family together for a family prayer, he assured them that God loves His Children and will always take care of them. So, after they heard the encouraging prayer that Pastor Gerald led them through, the family was more relieved. When John was notified about his Nephew, he started weeping for David and all the family. No matter how different Bob and his family were, when in trouble they stuck together. He loved David like his own Son. John realized how close both families were. When he got to the Hospital, he was relieved that David was going to pull through.

John didn't understand how God works and how he is always in control. So, to emphasize one more time, Roman8:28" We know that God causes all things to work together for good to those that love God" He couldn't understand how why the Lords servants have to go through trials and tribulations. He started wondering why this happened to such a devoted family. He could not understand that Jesus made the ultimate sacrifice, Phil:1:29" says that it has been granted us on behalf of Christ not only to believe in him, but to suffer for Him" Bob had to explain to John that God allows us to be tested so that our Faith in Him can get stronger. John, we have the faith that we are going to be stronger after our little setback. Bob I can't understand why when you are so devoted in serving God bad things are happening to your family. Bob, I don't mean that you should stop serving God, but you must understand that your family come first You have to protect your business for your family's sake. John if you read 2nd Cor. Says that God blesses us in all our needs. God will always bless us no matter what obstacles we face. No matter what happens we must continue our Mission.

Chapter Ten

"John's Concern For Bob Neglecting His Business"

SINCE DAVID WAS unable to do much his brothers Brian and Robert were busy with the ministry, he will always be in prayer for the ministry to continue without interruption. Phil 4:19" And my God will supply all our needs according to His riches and Glory in Christ Jesus" When the Ministry workers heard what happened to David they became more united in being the salt of the Earth. People from all around the community were donating food, furniture and clothing. Volunteers were busy finding needy people to donate the food and clothing. The refrigerators were full of food. Since the Bob and his family were so busy with the Lords work. They didn't have time to tend to the family business. Psalm 108:13" With God we will do mighty things, for He will trample down our foes" John looked around he noticed that Bob and his family were so busy with their Ministry that they ignored everything else around them. Bob was not concerned because he knew that the Lord is on their side. since They were having their employees taking care of the business. It was noticeable that the business was being neglected. Having their employees in charge was not enough. Bob realized that he had to have a relative in charge, so he appointed his Daughter Rose to oversee their business. Even though John found out that Bob put Rose in

Charge of running the business, he was very concerned that the rest of the family were too involved in their mission work, so he decided to have a talk with his brother.

Just because you are so devoted to serving the Lord my brother you are willing to lose everything, it will be to late when you realize what a mistake you are making. Not only B&J dairy farm is being less productive, but J&B trucking company is losing business. John look around you, you can see the progress we've made, we can't let anything interfere with our Ministry of helping our Brothers and Sisters. John our parents taught us to be compassionate to the less fortunate. I pray that Christ and the Holy Spirit will make you realize that the Lord needs you to become one of His servants, so poverty can be stamped out in our community and World. Phil.3:13 "Brethren I do not regard myself as having laid hold of it yet; but one thing I do forgetting what lies behind and reaching forward to what lies ahead" So we are to forget what is behind us and keep on moving forward.

John I'm concerned about my business. I know that our business would be more productive if we forget our promise to God, but if we were to turn back and forget what has been accomplished so many people would be devastated. We are the light of hope for our less fortunate Brothers and Sisters. John if I turn back and look at what I'm leaving behind I'll be like Lots wife and turn into a pillar of salt. My brother I'm not worried about what's happening with our business, because God is in control, and he will see that we have everything we need. Math6:26" tells us that the birds do not sow, reap or store food in barns, but God takes care of them, and we are much better than the birds" That is why our faith in God will take care of our business.

With their handicap Rebecca and David are concerned about their future, but with the Grace of God they will have their faith to prevail. 2nd Cor11:23-28 tells us how Paul suffered but kept on with his ministry. We are to use Paul as an example and keep on doing the Lords work. God chose us to be the light of the world, we cannot turn back.

Chapter Eleven

"More Trails For Bob's Family"

ONE DAY WHILE we were having a lot of success doing the Lords work, we got word that we were having problems with B&J farm. Jake the dairy Forman informed us that the barns needed a lot of repair, and about half our cows were not producing milk due to nutritional deficiencies. Since the income from the farm was down by fifty percent, we are losing customers and when we do I'm afraid they will never come back to us and we will start losing money. Bob assigned Brian to help Rose see what to do to resolve the issue.

It took John a few days to find out about the issues with the dairy farm, but when he found out he started wondering about what Bob was thinking. He was very concerned and disturbed, so he went to Bobs office and had a long conversation with Bob. Bob will you stop and listen to me, even though the farm belongs to the family, we must figure out how to modernize the farm, so it will become more productive. Bob you are neglecting your business just to help people you don't even know. I'm sure they need help, but other people can take over. Bob the Government has many programs, they can take over that's why we pay taxes. Are all this people your helping going to stand with you when you go under. Are you going to lose everything to fulfill your promise to God? Brother you better wake up, it's not too late to save your Estate. John my brother it doesn't matter what we go through our commitment to God is going to be fulfilled. God has a plan for us, he has a plan for you too. Mathew 6:31-32-33" 32" Do not be anxious saying, what shall we eat? or what shall we drink? Or with what shall we cloth ourselves? 33,For all this thing the Gentiles eagerly seek; for your Heavenly Father knows that you need all this things but seek first His Kingdom and His righteousness and all this things shall be added to you" John you might think you're doing fine, but you don't realize that earthly riches are nothing when you receive riches from Heaven. You must make God the center of your life.

John still didn't understand that God never goes back on His promises. Bob remember how hard our parents worked so we could have a productive future. He reminded Bob that if he didn't change his mind the Andrew family is going to lose everything John please understand that when we labor for the Lord, with our faith He is going to see that we fulfill our promise. I have no doubt that at the end He is going to send His blessings.

"Lord may your unfailing love be our comfort"

Chapter Twelve

"More Trails For David"

IT WAS ABOUT ten pm when David went to bed. It had been a few months that he was released from the Hospital. He Was having a very slow recovery. Some days he felt like he was making progress, and other days he was depressed because his progress was very slow. He had a lot of discomfort with his cast. He Just before he went to bed he was complaining that he didn't feel too good. About five am the next day, David woke up with a lot of pain in his leg. Bob and Rebecca could hear him moaning and yelling. When they came to his room they found him sweating and crying with pain. While Bob checked his leg, Because of his cast the only thing exposed were his toes and they looked blue. Rebecca called the paramedics. When the Paramedics arrived the first thing they did was sedate him, and then examined his leg and decided that he had to go to the Hospital. Bob rode in the Ambulance with his son. On the way Bob was praying and encouraging David reminding him that Jesus will always be with him. As he was praying he was also begging God to spare his son. He has already taken his parents he didn't want to lose his son. It would be devastating to lose his son. Parents are not supposed to bury their children. After arriving at the Hospital David felt a little better because he could feel the love his family had for him. After going through several test's, it was determined that he has a bone infection. The future doesn't look good for David. The Doctors determined that if he didn't respond to antibiotics his leg would have to be amputated. The news was devastating for the whole family. The future didn't look good for David, the only hope was that God was always with him and He will pull him through. Two days after David was Hospitalized, the family Lawyer informed them that the couple that were involved with David's accident decided to sue David for their injuries. After thinking it over Bob decided to contact David's insurance. That's when they got more bad news. Because David was so excited about the progress being made with their Ministry, he forgot to pay his insurance. His insurance had been canceled. Since David was at fault for the accident, it is going to cost a lot of money to settle with the couple. David was so devastated that Bob had to call Pastor Gerald. Pastor Gerald assured David and the family that God is on their side, and he will not leave them or forsake them. The whole family needed counseling. The Pastor assured them that they are not alone. 1st Peter5:6-7 tells us that we are to humble ourselves unto the mighty hand of God. We are to cast our problems on Him because He cares for us. 2nd cor.1:3-5 says that we are rely on God because He is the God of all comfort He comforts us in all our troubles.

When John came to see David, he saw his nephew suffer and he started to weep. John loved his Nephew liked he loved his own sons. he looked at the family with a lot of sorrow. Bob I'm so sorry for what is happening to you and your family. Bob you are my brother and when you suffer my family and I suffer too. Why don't we figure some way of you tending to your business, and not putting your family in jeopardy? Brother the saying goes that God helps those that help themselves. Yes John, but you must ask for his blessings too. My family and I are going to trust in God. At the end we are going to be victorious.

We thank you for your concern John my dear brother, but God is on our side and He will provide all our needs. When Paul was in distress God was by his side. No matter what we face we will struggle on. At the end He will send us His Blessings. No matter what we face we will struggle on. Again, John thank you for your concern, but when God is on our side I am not worried nothing can go wrong. He will provide all our needs. Christ himself asked God that if it was possible to let his cup pass from Him, but he did His Fathers will. No matter what it looks like now, at the end we will be victorious.

Chapter Thirteen

"John's Concern For Bob's Business"

WHILE THE ANDREW family were having a lot of success with the Ministry. Psalm 50:14-15" 14. Offer to God a sacrifice of thanksgiving and pay your vows to the highest. 15. And call upon Me in the day of trouble; I shall rescue you and you will honor Me" As John was tending to his own business, he was worried that his brother and family were neglecting their business's and were starting to lose money or barely surviving. Bob noticed how John was worried for him and his family. My brother I am not worried because God has us under His wing. With God leading us we are having so much success that we cannot slow down. We are in the process of building low income homes and new homeless shelters. The area Churches are proving scholarships for low income Students. We are ministering to many people and telling them that God is Love and they must depend on Him. The more we obey the Lord and do His work the more blessings we get from Him. Luke6:36" Be merciful just as your Father is merciful" I tell you John, you have to depend on our Redeemer. He thought that by being on his own God will bless him, but he must understand that God is the giver of all. the more we give the more blessings are given to us. God Blesses a cheerful giver. John did not understand the miracles of God. Since he did not understand what faith is. He was afraid that his brother's family are going to lose everything.

Bob informed John that we walk by faith. We know that Gods blessings are going to fill our lives, so all we must do is obey Him and he will give us shelter.

It was Monday morning when David's Lawyer informed us that the couple that sued David decided to settle for two million dollars. We had to go into our savings fund to pay the settlement. We had to sell some oil stock to replenish our reserve. Along with the bad news Bob got some good news. Their friends Roy and Liz found out that Bob loves dogs, so they presented Bob with a small little gray dog. The dog was so small and cute that he named him Chico.

Chapter Fourteen

"John Takes Control Of Bobs Business"

EVEN THOUGH WE were having so much success with the Ministry, we knew that God was giving us so many Blessings, but we got bad news about our business's. The dairy farm was in bad shape also J&B trucking was starting to lose money. Over half the trucks were much need of repair. Some of our steady customers were going to other companies. The problems with the businesses were getting out of control. John was so worried that Bob was going to lose everything. He knew that if Bob went under he would go under with him, so he decided to take matters into his own hands. He was angry as he stormed into Bobs office. He confronted Bob by reminding him that the businesses were going under. Bob, I have to let you know that I will temporarily take control until the businesses start being productive again. Bob asked God for direction and even though things are going to be fine, he decided to let his brother temporarily take over. Since his uncle was going to take over, Brian decided to help his uncle, which means that Robert was on his own with the warehouse. Bob and his family also found out that Rebecca is not feeling good. She gets dizzy spells and is always feeling weak. Her Doctor had to double her insulin because her sugar was out of control. She was very frustrated because she can't fulfill her duties.

Luke 6:35" But love your enemies, and do good and lend, expecting nothing in return, and your rewards will be great, and you will be sons; for He Himself is kind to ungrateful and evil men" It looked like Satan was trying to challenge us by putting obstacles to keep us from our commitment, but with our faith and the Holy Spirit He is not going to defeat us. Members of our Church decided to step in and help us. With their help things got a little easier. John didn't understand what was going on, so he decided to criticize Bob and his family. Since John didn't understand what faith is, he thought the whole Ministry is going to fail. John is a very negative person. He didn't understand that God is in control and is always on our side. Psalm 55:22-23 says to cast our burden upon the Lord, and He will never suffer the Righteous to be moved. He will always sustain us and never allow us to be shaken. James Chapter one states that when we have trouble of any kind we are to consider it a great joy. When our faith is tested our endurance has a chance to grow.

Chapter Fifteen

"Work For The Lord Doing Great"

EVEN THOUGH WE were having problems and John took control of the businesses. Bob still had access to the financial side of the family holdings. The Ministry still needed monetary help to keep it going. Even though John was handling the family's businesses he still needed to remind Bob that too much money was going to the Ministry and not enough to the businesses. Bob had the faith that God was taking care of both business and Ministry. John did not understand that when God is with us who can be against us. Our work for the Lord was going great. God was blessing us with hundreds of volunteers that we decided to break ground for low income homes which will be located on part of the one hundred and fifty acres donated by the Andrew family. To finance the project, Bob had to sell part of our oil stocks. When John heard that we were selling some oil stocks he was furious. Bob what in the world is happening to you what are you thinking? Who is going to come to your rescue when you lose everything? I don't see how you will be able to help poor people when you will be as poor as they are. John your lack of faith makes me more determined to prove to you that the Lord will not leave us or forsake us.

Even though Rebecca was full of faith, she was worried that we were using too much of our wealth to finance a lot of our projects. What if John was right and we lose everything. It looked like

Rebecca's faith was beginning to crumble. David got some good news. His Doctor informed that his leg was healing, He was glad that soon he will be able to help the family, but it will take some time to fully recover. When John found out that there was still too much money was being used, he thought that the whole world was going to collapse on Bobs family, But Bob is not worried, he knows that their faith is going to pull them through.

Even though John grew up being a believer, he didn't understand what faith is. Everything Bob did was by Faith. He knew that God was leading him, and through faith he was getting things done. John didn't understand that Bob is obeying God because he was chosen to be part of the salt of the Earth. Bob is going to do Gods will, because he has the faith that at the end he is going to be victorious. Bob explained to John that faith releases fears, and that is why he is not afraid to carry on.

Even though the Andrew family knew they had to walk by faith and the Lord was leading them, all but Bob were beginning to have doubts. Proverbs three five says" to trust on the Lord with all your heart, and do not lean on your own understanding" When Satan brings doubts on believer's minds, they lose faith that God is going to see them through all their difficulties. Johns negative attitudes were beginning to effect Bobs family. His wife Rebecca, and son David and daughter Rose were started to question their Fathers Faith. Satan was using Johns attitude as an instrument to cast doubts on the family, but no matter what John thought about knew that at the end with God the battle will be won. John even though you think we are going to lose everything, Satan will not touch us. All we have to do is tell Satan what Christ told him when he was in the wilderness.

Even though Bob and his family were having so much success doing the Lords work, things didn't look good with their finances. The dairy farm was not doing well. The oil prices were down by sixty percent. When John heard about the oil prices he couldn't believe that Bob was not worried. John was so worried about his brother that he had to confront him. Bob, I don't know what's going to happen the way things are going. When are you going

I Remembered Job

to realize that if things don't change you are in danger of going into Bankruptcy? Our parents made sure that we would always be financially secured. Even though God is always going to be with Bob and his family, his family's faith is beginning to falter. Bob remembered Isaiah 26:4" trust in the Lord forever, for the Lord God is an everlasting rock" So, Bobs faith is solid like the house that was built upon the rock.

God is allowing Satan to test Bob and his family.

Chapter Sixteen

"The Beginning Of Bob's Family Turning On Him"

BOB AND HIS family were celebrating the fourth of July. They invited John and his family. It was a nice New Mexico summer day. There were clouds gathering from the east. It looked that there was going to be a New Mexico summer storm with thunder and lightning, but both families were enjoying the holiday. Bob was happy to see the whole family enjoy the day. Since things were not going right, Bobs family decided to have a discussion with him. Bob didn't realize that the family was so concerned about the family businesses. Rebecca was the first to speak. Bob my honey I love you and I know that what your doing is to Glorify God, but I have to let you know that I'm worried about our finances. Our source of income is in jeopardy. We have to pay more attention to our business's. More money is going out then coming in. After a long pause, David was the next to speak. Dad Brian is busy helping Uncle John with the trucking company. Robert is running the warehouse by himself and he needs help. I see him struggle but there is little I can do to help. My Mom is having problems with her health. John was the next to speak. Bob my brother I'm worried for you. When are you going to realize that everything around you is collapsing? Bob I'm so frustrated that I'm starting to question the existence of God.

Bob stared at the sky with disbelief, John I can't believe what came out of your mouth. The Bible say in psalm14-1" the fool has in his heart there is no God" My brother don't you Remember when we were growing up our parents taught about the Lord. We learned that Christ died for our sins. John, I know that you are no fool, so before we continue this conversation, you have to ask God to forgive you. It crushes my heart to hear what came out of my brothers' mouth. God loves us so much that he sends His Son to shed His Blood, so we can say we are saved. Bob I'm sorry for what I said, I do believe. John was so sorry for what he said, he began to weep. I know that God will forgive me, but I love you and I'm worried for you and your family. John, I know you care, but my promise to God must be fulfilled. I know that we are going to go through a lot of trails, but the Lord will see us through them. The Apostle Paul did not waver when He went through His trails

23 Psalm

"The lord is my shepherd I shall not want. He makes me lie down in green pastures. He leads me beside the still waters. He restores my soul. He leads me in the path of righteousness for His name sake. Yea though I walk through the valley of the shadow of death, I will fear no evil; for thou art with me, thy rod and thy staff they will comfort me, thou prepare a table before me in the presence of my enemies. Thou anoint my head with oil, my cup runs over. Surely goodness and mercy shall fallow me all the days of my life, and I will dwell in the house of the Lord forever"

Chapter Seventeen

"The Testing Of Bob's Faith"

AS HE WAS seeing the blessings of God, Bob was sorry to see his family concerned about the way things were going and seeing how the businesses were being neglected. But Bob was not worried. He knew that at the end Gods love is going to prevail. Even though the ministry was going great the businesses were not doing well, but Bob knew that at the end God is going to restore everything. Bob prayed that his family's faith remains strong.

One day as Bob looked around him, he started thinking that the more Satan was making things difficult for him the closer he got to God. To clear his mind, he decided to go for a walk. It looked like the only friend, he had was his little dog Chico, so he put him on a leach and took him along. As he was going on his walk he started asking God for guidance. My Lord I know that we are to let you guide our lives and You will take care of us, but my family is beginning to question their faith in You. No matter what happens Lord I will not turn back. I will always have faith in You. You will never let go on my own. Just lead the way and reveal to me what I must do. My faith will never waiver.

When Bob and Chico returned from their walk, his family along with Johns family were waiting for him. They decided to have a meeting to discuss their finances. John informed Bob that their bank has contacted them. They were informed that they have to put more capital in order to meet their obligations. Too much money is coming out and it is not being replaced. Brian was the next to speak. Dad our Mom is getting more and more concerned, and it's not helping her diabetes. Her Doctor had to double her insulin. David is so depressed because there is little he can do to help. Dad were afraid that the way things are going we might have to file for Bankruptcy. We must liquidate some of our stocks in order to replenish our bank assets. Even though the oil prices were at an all-time low they, still had a lot of capital, but is was getting low. We decided that with your blessing to let Uncle John take control of the businesses. John my brother if my family and you think that it's the best way to go, you have my blessing, but I still need capital continue the Ministry. I will not abundant my promise to God. It was obvious that the family was not content with Bob. So, they concluded that they are going to give John the power of Attorney to oversee all the Andrew family's finances. So, John decided to give Bob enough for his living expenses. Bob was disappointed that his family disowned him. So, he realized that he's all alone, but God is still on his side. I will find ways to continue the Ministry even if I have to find a job I'll continue the Ministry Even though I know that I'm all alone, I know that God is with me. I'm going to find ways to continue Gods work. My mind is made up I have faith that my Lord will provide. The more obstacles Satan puts against me the stronger my faith gets. Moses had so much faith that he led his people out of Egypt.

Chapter Eighteen

"Bob Defends God's Mercies"

AFTER THE DECISION was made to let John take over the business's, even though he agreed with the decision, and that God is in control, Bob felt alone and isolated. He was sad that his family forgot about the power of God and lost all their faith. He decided to go into his office to see if in seclusion he can ask for direction and pray that his family will once again come to realize that with God on their side nothing can go wrong. He went outside to breath some fresh air. Chico went with him. He knew that no matter what happens Chico will be on his side. He noticed what a happy little dog he was, but we have to understand that human life is a lot more complicated. We were formed in the image of God, but by Adam and Eve's sin by disobeying God we must live by their decision. Christ had to come shed his blood and die on the cross to have our sins forgiven.

Bob took Chico and went for a walk. On his walk he started looking back at his life. He remembers that even when he was a small Child his dream was to always be a servant for the Lord. He was always full of compassion for the less fortunate and was involved in helping people in the community. He was grateful that since he was a little boy, his parents led him to the path that leads to salvation. After thinking how much he has done and all that has happened in his life, there is no way he can turn his Back on God 1st Samuel 12:24" says fear the Lord and serve Him faithfully with all your heart consider what things He has done for you" He loves us so much that He sent His Son to pay the price, and all we have to do is fallow Him. Father even though I find myself alone I know You will never leave me or forsake me, and I will fallow You where ever you lead me. Lord You blessed our family with a lot of wealth, Father I know we still have enough wealth to continue our Ministry, but they forgot that You are a God of compassion and it is You who gives us everything. Everything belongs to You. What is the benefit of having riches on earth and lose our souls. The Bible says that its easier for a camel to go through the eye of a needle then for a rich man to be saved.

Lord looking back thirty-two years that You took my parents. It was hard, but it is in Your plan. I know that you have a plan for us and with Your leadership and guidance my family will be victorious. I pray that my family will eventually see that our work was not in vain. Lord eventually You will give us an abundance of Blessings, all we have to do is keep on being faithful.

Chapter Nineteen

"The Turnaround"

IT HAS BEEN forty-five years that Bob, and Johns parents Richard and Sara met and got married. Bob had a lot of memories most were good memories, and he was glad that God was always on his side. When Bob came back from his walk, he decided to go somewhere to be closer to God. So, he decided to go to his family retreat for a few weeks to be away from all disturbances. Since he had no way of getting money it took every dollar he had left to buy provisions and to fill his cars gas tank. He took little Chico with him. Bob was thinking how God had blessed the family, but he was afraid his family had stopped trusting Him. He thought that with Prayer and Fasting the Holy Spirit will intervene and make them understand that when they leave God from being the center of their lives eventually they are going to fail, but if they obey Him they will be full of Blessings. About a month after Bob went on seclusion, John started noticing that some things were beginning change. Since John had control of the businesses he decided to make some improvements. He modernized the dairy farm and bought new equipment for the trucking company. Brian decided to put some bids on some construction job sites around the metro. David got good news about his leg. With therapy and medication his leg was healing fast. He didn't have to use his crushes any more. Even thou she missed her husband Rebecca is feeling much better now that she didn't have so much pressure. After months of working on the low-income homes over half were finished and occupied. The local Baptist Association decided to divert some of their Mission funds to help with the local endeavor. Rebecca and Mary noticed that more and more people were volunteering to help with homeless shelters. A lot of people were coming out of poverty.

About a month after John seeing changes around the businesses it dawned on him that things were improving all around him. He started thinking about his brother, so he went to his office and started praying for Bob. It had been fifty-two years that his Father had moved from Wisconsin to Albuquerque met and married his Mom and conceived us. Ever since I can remember, my brothers' goal was to help the less fortunate. The more John thought about his brother the guiltier he felt for questioning his intentions. He loved Bob and his family and will do everything to help them. He felt sorry for relieving Bob from all family legal matters. He thought about the many things Bob had done for the poor people in the community. He thought Bob was the kindest person he has ever known. After reminiscing about how wonderful things his brother had going. John was amazed at the progress being made with the homeless shelters. The motel they bought was converted into small apartment units and were occupied with formally homeless people. The low-income housing was going strong. Twenty home were finished and thirty are under construction. all with volunteer workers.

A month has past, and Bob is still in seclusion. John went into his office and to his surprise he found Brian waiting for him. Brian informed him that since they refurbished the trucking company, they won bids for several jobs. John and Brian decided since they were going to have so much work, they are going to have to hire more personal. We need about thirty new drivers plus we have to hire mechanics and office personal. Uncle why don't we hire needy people we've been helping. John thought it was a good idea. After training them we could take a lot of family's out of poverty. This will make Bob happy because all his work was not in vain. Two weeks later when John was in his office two oil executives payed him a visit. They informed him that oil was discovered in Southern New Mexico. This meant millions of dollars for Bob and Johns families.

I Remembered Job

They wanted to know if they could buy or lease their property. John couldn't give them an answer because he had to consult with Bob. As all this was going on John realized that Bob was right.

In the meantime, Bob had been in the family retreat for over a month. After weeks of prayer and fasting he knew that God had answered his prayers. After thanking God, he decided to go see how his family was doing. On his way home, he started praying that the Holy Spirit make the family realize that God needs them to do His work. Luke 10:2 says that the harvest is ready, but the workers are few. As he was driving he called ahead to let them know that he was on his way back. He didn't know what was waiting for him.

As he approached his house he noticed that the whole family was waiting for him. He didn't realize that they had some good news. When he came in after he hugged Rebecca he noticed that everybody was looking at him with tears in their eyes. John was the first to speak. As he started talking with tears in his eyes he informed Bob that he had nothing but good news for him. My brother you were right that God has always been on your side. All our businesses are prospering again David found out that his leg was completely healed. Your wife is feeling much better now that she is more relaxed. The homeless shelters are finished, and the low-income housing are almost finished. We have so many volunteers that they have to work in shifts, but best of all, Oil was discovered on our property in Southern New Mexico. We have to decide if we sell or lease the property. Now will have enough capital for you to continue the Ministry without interruption. But the biggest news is that God was always on your side. Bob were so sorry for interfering with your promise to God. Honey your sons' daughters and I ask you to forgive us for doubting you. We will be with you from now on working for the Lord. With our new revenues we will be able to help more people We will be on fire for the Lord.

Proverbs One

"Blessed is the one who perseveres under trail, because having stood the test, that person will receive the crown of life that the Lord has promised to those who love Him"

Chapter Twenty

"Bob's Victory Lap"

NINETEEN MONTHS AFTER the miraculous turn around with the Andrew family, everything was looking up. Thousands of people were being helped. The family wealth grew by sixty percent. Bob was so grateful that God was always on his side and granted him everything he asked for, that he decided to let people know how He uses us as His tools to care for His people. It was one Sunday evening when Bob was invited to tell his story. He got the family together along with people from the community. to remind them how God Blesses those who serve Him. He started by reminding them that God created them, Rev. 14:11" Worthy art thou, our Lord and our God, to receive glory and honor and power; for thou did create all things, and of thy will they existed, and were created God created us for His own pleasure. "Genesis 1:27" and God created man in His own Image, in the image of God He created him male and female He created them" While Adam and Eve were living in the Garden they decided to disobey God, and since then sin started. God gave men many chances to repent. He had Prophets try and turn them from Evil, but men kept on sinning. He sent His Son born of a Virgin. Jesus lived a sinless Life. He Preached love and repentance He was arrested, they beat Him whipped Him. He was nailed to the Cross. He died and in three days He conquered death. He Ascended to Heaven, and He sent the Holy Spirit to be our guide. Now what we must love one another. That is why it's so important to obey and fallow Him. If we obey Him He will lead us in a path of righteousness. When obey Him, He will never leave us or forsake us. If we care for our Fellow men we will never go wrong, for He will always Love us and protect us. It took a while for my family to find out that with God all things are possible.

Bob was so happy that his family saw what it is to live by faith. Look at what the Lord has done for us. 1 Corinthians 13:3 "And if I gave all my possessions to feed the poor, and if I deliver my body to be burned, but do not have love, it profits me nothing." This is why so many people have been helped, and for all we did He gave us more abundantly, and He poured His blessings on us. John starred at his brother saying brother I will not doubt you anymore. I can't thank my Lord enough for you being my brother and also part of my life. Bob, I can say you are a modern-day Job. "AMEN".

THE END

www.ingramcontent.com/pod-product-compliance
Lightning Source LLC
Chambersburg PA
CBHW071916070526
44583CB00016B/2012